Out of this World

Thanks to Jane
for her love and
no-nonsense advice

To Tim Snowdon
for the photo on the back

*And to the following
for their excellent
editorial advice*

Jane Blazeby
Sue Doggett
Pete Halestrap
Jane Norman
Anna Williams

Lightning BOLTS

OUT OF THIS WORLD

Nick Jones

The Bible Reading Fellowship
OPENING THE BIBLE

Published by
The Bible Reading Fellowship
Peter's Way, Sandy Lane West
Oxford, England
ISBN 0 7459 3083 2
Albatross Books Pty Ltd
PO Box 320, Sutherland
NSW 2232, Australia
ISBN 0 7324 0940 3

First edition 1995
10 9 8 7 6 5 4 3 2 1 0

Acknowledgments

Unless otherwise stated, scripture is quoted from the **Good News Bible**, published by The Bible Societies/HarperCollins Publishers Ltd., UK, © American Bible Society, 1966, 1971, 1976, 1992

The Holy Bible, New International Version (NIV), © 1973, 1978, 1984 by International Bible Society. Used by permission.

Cover photograph: Zefa UK

A catalogue record for this book is available from the British Library

Printed and bound in Great Britain
by Cox and Wyman Ltd, Reading

Welcome to Out of This World . . .

These daily Bible readings take you on a lightning tour of ten crunch moments in God's master plan for the disaster-prone human race. Spanning the entire Bible they investigate . . .

- Why God made the two-eyed, thirty-two-toothed human being.
- Why he washed the human race out of his hair.
- What God was up to when he put on nappies.
- Why God's 'new heart' treatment makes all the difference.
- How *you* can help God clinch his master plan once and for all.

The plan of the Master in the face of disaster is a heart-warming tale of love that is truly 'out of this world'. These daily readings will help you to explore it for yourself.

Each day's reading includes an introduction to the passage, thought provoking thoughts or activities to help you get your mind round its meaning, as well as things to pray about or ponder. For each reading I have written out the key verse just in case you don't have time to read the whole passage.

Getting Going

Each day find yourself a quiet spot where you won't be disturbed for five minutes or so. This can be at any time of the day or night. I find that before breakfast is best, but you may prefer to do your reading on the bus into school, in the bath, or in bed. Settle down with your Bible, this book and a biro and turn to Day One's reading. Ask God to help you understand the passage and then follow the instructions on the page. When you've finished you can tick the box next to the day number. If you ever have trouble finding the passage in the Bible, look it up in the contents page at the beginning of your Bible.

I hope that you really enjoy exploring the plan of the Master in the face of disaster. I did and found it to be truly out of this world.

Nick

The voice of the Lord speaks with flashes of lightning.

Psalm 29:7 (NIV)

Contents

Off To A Grand Start

You may not be surprised to hear that the plan of the Master starts at the beginning, and the beginning is where we're going to start our investigation. So get ready to wind your clocks back billions and billions of years, even to before the beginning of time (if that were possible). And prepare to discover why God made the two-eyed, thirty-two-toothed human being.

In the beginning

Read: Genesis 1 verses 1–5

In the beginning, when God created the universe, the earth was formless and desolate. The raging ocean that covered everything was engulfed in total darkness, and the Spirit of God was moving over the water.

Genesis 1:1–2

In the beginning, before God created the universe, God was all there was; God was everywhere and there was nothing but God; no time, no matter, no trees, no anything; just God. God decided amongst himself that he was going to embark on a very special project. He was going to have a bit of fun creating a sensational universe and top it off by filling it with two-eyed, thirty-two-toothed human beings with whom he could have an extra-special relationship. That is the plan of the Master in a nutshell.

Ponder this

Why not invent a conversation between God and himself as he devises his master plan?

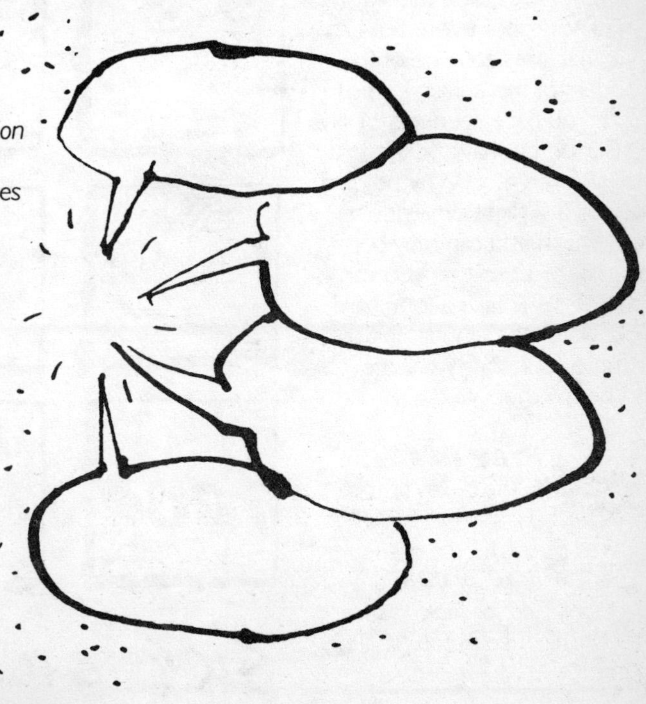

2

Skies galore

Read: Genesis 1 verses 6–8

God made a dome, and it separated the water under it from the water above it. He named the dome 'Sky'. Evening passed and morning came—that was the second day.

Genesis 1:7b–8

In the first seven days of these readings we will look at the seven stages of God's creation of the universe. (Just in case you were wondering, the Genesis story of creation is not a scientific textbook account of 'how' God made the world in 144 hours. It is more like a seven verse poem describing why God made the world and what he feels about it.)

Anyway, onto 'Stage Two' of creation. God made the sky. I don't know about you, but I think that skies are one of the wonders of the universe. No doubt you have seen lots of sky in your life but have you ever really looked at it? Why not find yourself a skylight or window from which you can only see the sky, (or sit so that you can only see sky). Take a long hard look; watch the clouds drift by or the colour slowly change and be mind-boggled.

Pray this

In the boxes of this sky chart draw (with coloured pencils) some of the different kinds of sky there are and thank God for making such a technicolour backdrop for life on earth.

SKY CHART

Land ahoy!

Read: Genesis 1 verses 9–13

Then God commanded, 'Let the water below the sky come together in one place, so that land will appear'—and it was done. He named the land 'Earth', and the water which had come together he named 'Sea'. And God was pleased with what he saw.

Genesis 1:9–10

The things that God made in 'Stage Three' of creation really send a t-i-i-i-i-ngle down my spine: land, sea and vegetation. So much so that I spend most of my time painting pictures of land, water and plants. I am absolutely hooked on being outside, whether walking up wild hills, watching reflections or looking at tiny clumps of moss covered in dew. When I get back to the studio I try and paint what it felt like being out in the landscape. Call me weird, but I really think the things that God made in 'Stage Three' are sensationally beautiful. I'm not surprised God was 'pleased' with them—I would have been over the moon!

Ponder this

Why not wander outside, find yourself a leaf or flower and really look at it? Stick your bit of vegetation in the specimin pot and write a note to God about how it makes you feel. If it really boggles your mind perhaps you could even paint a picture to him about it!

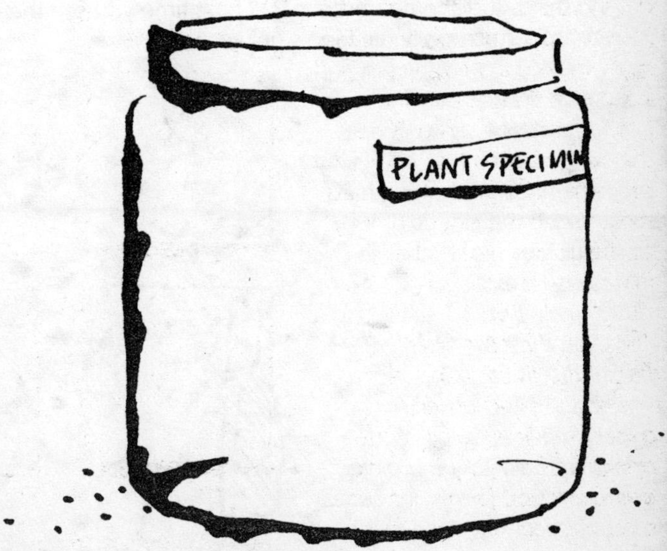

On the large side

Read: Genesis 1 verses 14–19

God made two larger lights, the sun to rule over the day and the moon to rule over the night; he also made the stars.

Genesis 1:16

If you go outside on a really clear night you can see hundreds of thousands of tiny points of light dotted all over the sky—stars. These stars give us a little glimpse of how enormous the universe is. Try and get your mind round these facts:

- Distances in space are measured in 'light years'—that is the distance light travels in a year. Light travels at 300,000 km per second. That is four times round the earth every second. Pretty fast, eh?
- The light from the sun takes eight minutes to travel the 150 million km to planet earth and 5 hours to reach us from Pluto, the furthest planet in our solar system.
- The nearest star to earth is called 'Alpha Centurae' and its light (travelling at 300,000 km per second) takes a full *four years and four months* to reach us! And that is just the nearest star! So next time you see the night sky remember how jolly big God's universe is.

Pray this

Dear God, when I think about how enormous the universe is I feel rather small. But thank you that the universe is so big and so amazing and thank you that your love for me is even bigger.

Animal magic

Read: Genesis 1:20–25

Then God commanded, 'Let the water be filled with many kinds of living beings, and let the air be filled with birds.'

Genesis 1:20

The animal kingdom is quite out of this world. God has got a great imagination and a mellow sense of humour. Fancy being able to think up animals like giraffes, slugs and three-toed sloths. Anyway, put your animal knowledge to the test, get your watch out and see how quickly you can knock together a complete animal alphabet.

A	**J**	**S** ....
B	**K**	**T** ....
C	**L**	**U** ....
D	**M**	**V** ....
E	**N**	**W** ....
F	**O**	**X** ....
G	**P**	**Y** ....
H	**Q**	**Z** ....
I	**R**	

Don't worry if you had trouble with X because there aren't any animals beginning with X that I can think of. Anyway, how long did it take?

under 1 min—*you're an animal encyclopaedia*
1–5 mins—*you're an animal addict*
5–30 mins—*you're animal aware*
30–600 mins—*you're very determined*

Pray this

Thank God for a wonderful animal world.

Master piece?

Read: Genesis 1 verses 26–31

Then God said, 'And now we will make human beings; they will be like us and resemble us'... He created them male and female.

Genesis 1:26–27

At the end of 'Stage Six' God was 'very pleased' with everything he had made, and in particular with human beings. His master plan had gone according to plan. But what was it that made the two-eyed, thirty-two-toothed human being special and so different from cows, dogs, potatoes or anything else he had made? Well, it is to do with the fact that God made humans 'to be like himself'. That doesn't mean that God has legs, eyes and fingers but rather that we have the potential to behave in the same way as he does. Like God we can show love and forgiveness, be creative, have relationships, think and make plans. In a nutshell God made us to care about the same kind of things as he does, and to have a special relationship with him. What a plan!

Michelangelo painted a very famous picture of God making the first human being. It looks rather like this. In the speech bubble write something that God might have said to the first human about how he wanted him to behave.

Day off

Read: Genesis 2 verses 1–4

And so the whole universe was completed. By the seventh day God had finished what he had been doing and stopped working.

Genesis 2:1–2

By the end of 'Stage Six' God had finished creating the universe so 'Stage Seven' was going to be set aside for a well-deserved rest. God's master plan had got off to a grand start. Look back over God's handiwork in creating the world and write a school-type report on his efforts.

Pray this

Why not talk to God about what you have discovered over the last few days about his creation and why he made you?

Wash Out

The first disaster that the Master had to face is already upon us. Instead of being friends with God human beings turned their backs on him and went seriously off the rails, until the vast majority were only thinking and doing evil all the time. Things got so bad that God regretted ever making them and washed them out of his hair. But that wasn't the end because he started again with a man he could trust.

Trouble brewing

8

Read: Genesis 6 verses 5–7

When the Lord saw how wicked everyone on earth was and how evil their thoughts were all the time, he was sorry that he had ever made them and put them on the earth.

Genesis 6:5–6

Here is the first major disaster that the Master had to deal with—in fact, it is the disaster that recurs throughout the history of the world. The human race, instead of being good friends with God as he had planned, kicked him in the teeth and did their own thing which was evil 'all the time'. Bad news. In fact, a real disaster.

Try and put yourself in God's shoes. The Bible tells us that he was sorry that he had ever made human beings. What other feelings would he have had? Some suggestions are listed along the bottom of the bar chart below. For each one draw in a bar showing how much of that emotion you think he would have felt.

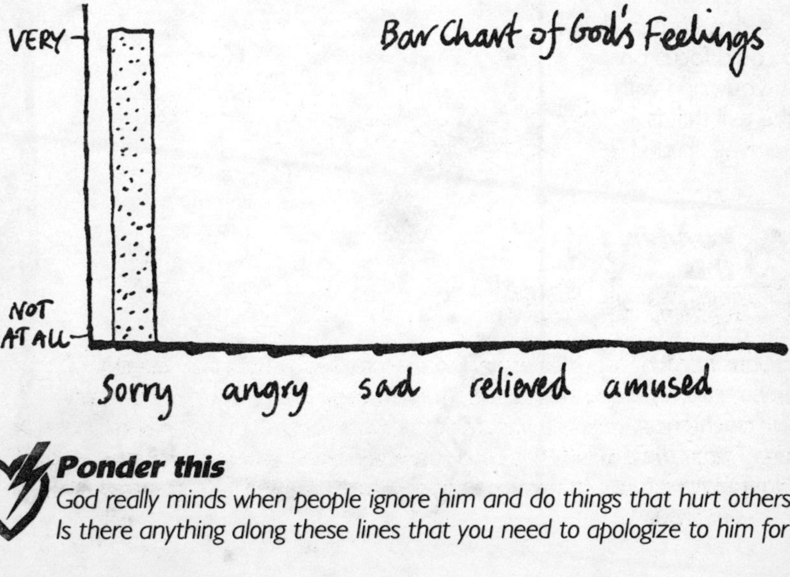

Ponder this

God really minds when people ignore him and do things that hurt others. Is there anything along these lines that you need to apologize to him for?

9

One in a million

Read: Genesis 6 verses 8–12

The Lord was pleased with Noah... Noah had no faults and was the only good man of his time. He lived in fellowship with God, but everyone else was evil in God's sight.

Genesis 6:8–11

In all the gloom of yesterday's passage there is one glimmer of hope—a good man called Noah. He was a friend of God when everyone else had made themselves his enemies.

It can't have been easy for Noah being so totally surrounded by people who did evil all the time. Imagine that you are Noah and write your diary entry for a typical day. Perhaps you could focus on how you cope with all the evil that is happening around you.

Ponder this

If you are one of only a few Christians in your school or class and find it tough being different from the rest then remember that Noah would know how you feel.

10

Drastic action

Read: Genesis 6 verse 13

God said to Noah, 'I have decided to put an end to the whole human race. I will destroy them completely, because the world is full of their violent deeds.'

Genesis 6:13

Well, the plan of the Master in the face of this first big disaster was pretty drastic. There was nothing for it but to wipe out all the people who did evil and start again with good old Noah. Sounds a bit excessive and not very loving, doesn't it? Well, I'm not so sure. Imagine that you are a modern day Dr Frankeinstein and have built yourself a robot to do your homework and keep your bedroom tidy. So long as your robot is working well all is fine, but if your little metal friend starts going hay-wire, trashing your bedroom, and making plans to blow up your school the only sensible thing to do would be switch it off—deactivate it before it does any more damage. That's a little bit like what happened in the flood. God's creations had gone hay-wire and were doing terrible damage and God had to switch them off.

Pray this

Dear God, it can't have been easy deciding to wipe out all the people that you had made, but if they really were only thinking and doing evil all time I suppose it was necessary. Help me to trust that you always know and do what is best, and to know and do it myself.

11

The plan

Read: Genesis 6 verse 14—Genesis 7 verse 5

God said to Noah, 'Build a boat for yourself… Go into the boat with your wife, your sons and their wives. Take into the boat with you a male and a female of every kind of animal and of every kind of bird, in order to keep them alive.'

Genesis 6:14, 18–20

Well, it's pretty obvious what God was planning to do. The crunch came when Noah decided whether to cooperate or not. If I had been in Noah's shoes I would have generally ***wanted*** to do what God asked, but probably would have wondered if I had heard him correctly. That wondering, along with a bit of negative peer-pressure might well have led me to scale down God's plan: 'Er, wouldn't building a lifeboat be a happy compromise God?' It wouldn't have been much use really.

Throughout these readings we will discover how God wants us to play a part in his master plan for the human race. Noah is the first good example for us to follow.

Ponder this

Have you ever felt that God wanted you to do something specific? What happened? Why not ask him to help you be more sure about what he wants you to do? **Hint:** *We know that God wants us to show love. So next time you are not sure if a certain course of action is what God wants, ask yourself the question, 'Is this a loving thing to do?' If the answer is 'no' it is unlikely to be what God wants you to do.*

12

Wash out

Read: Genesis 7 verses 6–24

The Lord destroyed all living beings on the earth—human beings, animals and birds. The only ones left were Noah and those who were with him in the boat.

***Genesis** 7:23*

Well, the rains came, the waters rose and only the inhabitants of the floating zoo were safe (and all fishes). Now, I'm sure that God knew what he was doing here, after all he is the almighty, totally loving and everlasting God. 'But,' I hear you ask, 'what about all those poor hamsters, lambs, monkeys and zebras who got drowned when the wickedness of the earth was nothing to do with them?' Well, it's a good question and I don't know what the answer is, except to say that God made the animals in the first place, he knows and loves them and I'm sure that he will make it up to them later.

Ponder this

The flood was the inevitable result of human selfishness. They brought it upon themselves and the whole world suffered the consequences. However, the environment is still suffering because of human selfishness; pollution, hunting whales and the destruction of the rainforests are all unnecessary. So, before you get too worked up about God wiping out the animals because of human sin, why not see what you can do to look after God's world a little bit more? Write it here.

....

....

....

Take two

Read: Genesis 8 verses 1–19

God said to Noah, 'Go out of the boat with your wife, your sons, and their wives. Take all the birds and animals out with you, so that they may reproduce and spread over all the earth.

Genesis 8:15–17

As God opened the door of the ark to let Noah and Co. out he must have thought to himself, 'Here we go again. Take two!' The human race had been given a fresh start and everything was looking rosy.

Ponder this

Imagine that you are Noah, pioneer of the future human race. You are very keen to get things off to a good start and help God's master plan to work out. What guidelines or rules would you set up for your family and their kids and future generations in order to prevent them from going off the rails? Jot down some notes for your landing speech to be delivered from the top of the ark's ramp.

The promise

Read: Genesis 9 verses 1–17

God said to Noah and his sons, 'I am now making my covenant with you and your descendants, and with all living beings—all birds and all animals... I promise that never again will all living beings be destroyed by a flood.'

Genesis 9:8–11

God made an agreement with Noah and all living beings. Never again would he destroy the world with a flood. Well, that's a relief! As a symbol of this agreement God put a rainbow in the sky as a reminder.

When I was a teenager I had a minor obsession with rainbows; rainbow stickers, rainbow pencils, rainbow laces, rainbow rainbows, (don't laugh, I'm sure you have your own funny little ways too). But the thing about rainbows, apart from looking stunning, is that they are a sign of hope. Out of the horror of the flood came the hope of a new start and that is the plan of the Master in the face of disaster through and through. He never gives up on us despite all we do. He is always ready to start again.

Pray this

Why not colour in the rainbow? As you do so, thank God that he never gives up on us.

PHASE THREE

Tipped For The Top

Unfortunately the descendants of Noah weren't all they might have been and God soon had the same kind of trouble on his hands again. What was he to do this time? Well, God reasoned that he would choose another person who walked closely with him and from this person's descendants build a special nation who would all walk closely with him. You may well think that God's chosen man wasn't the most suitable candidate for starting a large family as he was most definitely an OAP. But prepare to find out how Abraham fits into God's master plan.

Introducing Abram

Read: Genesis 11 verses 27–32

These are the descendants of Terah, who was the father of Abram... Abram married Sarai... Sarai was not able to have children... Terah took his son Abram... and his daughter-in-law Sarai, and with them he left the city of Ur in Babylonia to go to the land of Canaan.

Genesis 11:27, 29–31

Well, who is this Abram guy and what made him a likely candidate for a major role in the plan of the Master in the face of disaster? We will be finding out this week, but the raw family facts are in the passage. Imagine that you are a chat show host and that Abram is the guest on your show today. How would you introduce him to your audience? Write your opening blurb fitting in the facts of the passage.

The call

Read: Genesis 12 verses 1–3

The Lord said to Abram, 'Leave your country… and go to a land that I am going to show you. I will give you many descendants, and they will become a great nation. I will bless you and make your name famous, so that you will be a blessing.

Genesis 12:1–2

Wow, what a phone call! What would you have said if you got a call from God like that? Fill in the speech bubble.

Ponder this

God's plans are always master plans even if they do seem a bit difficult. After all, the prospect of leaving his lovely home and relatives and moving off into the desert can't have been that appealing to Abram.

But Abram trusted that God really loved him and knew what was best for him. And in the end things turned out just fine, surprise, surprise! That's a good lesson for us to learn too.

Taking the plunge

Read: Genesis 12 verses 4–9

When Abram was 75 years old, he started out from Haran, as the Lord had told him to do... Abram took his wife Sarai, his nephew Lot, and all the wealth and slaves he had acquired in Haran, and they started out for the land of Canaan.

Genesis 12:4–5

There was no pussy-footing around with Abram. God said it and Abram did it (and so did his whole family and household). Off into the desert they went. How do you react to the events described in this passage? Tick which ever box best describes your feelings.

- ☐ I'm amazed that Abram could hear God speaking to him in the first place.
- ☐ I'm surprised that Abram actually went.
- ☐ I'm jealous of Abram. Why doesn't God ever speak to me like that?
- ☐ I wonder if God gave him a map.
- ☐ Other ....

  ....

Pray this

Why not talk to God about the box you ticked and your feelings about Abram's experience?

Starry future

Read: Genesis 15 verses 1–6

The Lord took Abram outside and said, 'Look at the sky and try to count the stars; you will have as many descendants as that.' Abram put his trust in the Lord, and because of this the Lord was pleased with him and accepted him.

Genesis 15:5–6

Abram was feeling down. Maybe he'd had a bad day, or was getting fed up wandering the desert. Perhaps he was sad that Sarai wasn't able to have kids. Well, anyway, God showed up and told Abram to do some star-gazing; he was going to have that many descendants! Abram believed him.

The exciting thing about being a friend of God is that God can do the impossible and seems to quite enjoy it. So next time you are feeling down remember that as a friend of God you are on the side where the extraordinary happens.

Pray this

Why not talk to God about this and ask him to help you trust him a little bit more each day?

19

Heart to heart

Read: Genesis 18 verses 20–33

Abraham approached the Lord and asked, 'Are you really going to destroy the innocent with the guilty?...That is impossible! You can't do that!'... The Lord answered, 'If I find fifty innocent people in Sodom, I will spare the whole city for their sake.'

Genesis 18:23, 25–26

Here we get a glimpse of what it was that made Abram (now Abraham) so special. He cared passionately about justice and he talked to God as a friend talks to a friend.

Pray this

Abraham really cared about the innocent people of Sodom who were facing destruction because of the selfishness of the other Sodomites, and he bent God's ear on their behalf, begging him to spare them. Because of Abraham's prayer God allowed the innocent people to escape before he destroyed the city. Why not follow Abraham's example and pray about a situation in the world where people are suffering injustice? Just watch the news and you will get plenty of ideas. Why not use this space to write out your request to God? Follow Abraham's example and make it specific.

Seriously God...

It's a boy!

Read: Genesis 21 verses 1–8

The Lord blessed Sarah (Sarai), as he had promised, and she became pregnant and bore a son to Abraham when he was old... Abraham named him Isaac.

Genesis 21:1–3

'Have you heard the news? Who'd have thought it, eh? Old Abraham and his missis! Well-well-well, and it's a boy! Knocking on a hundred both of them. Well past it, I'd have thought! Quite amazing! But good luck to them I'd say!'

Ponder this

Have you ever wondered why God always seems to do things the hard way? Why did he have to wait till Abraham and Sarah were half dead before giving them the kid he'd promised? Maybe it is something to do with pride. When I do something well I tend to get all puffed up, but when something out of this world happens the only explanation is God. It was definitely God who gave Abraham and Sarah their baby—there was no other possible explanation.

21

Celestial babies

Read: Genesis 25 verses 19–26

Isaac was 40 years old when he married Rebecca… The time came for her to give birth and she had twin sons. The first one… was named Esau. The second one… was named Jacob.

Genesis 25: 20, 24–26

Abraham's son Isaac had two sons, Jacob and Esau. Jacob turned out to be the original baby boomer and had twelve sons as well as a daughter! The names of Abraham's great-grandsons are mentioned in the verses below. Look up each verse and write down the name of each child in the correct box. By reading down the central column you will find out what God wanted Abraham's descendants to be like.

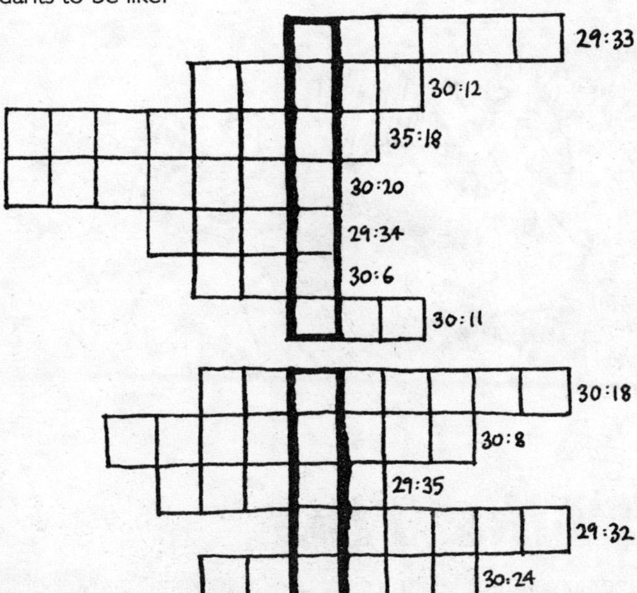

Ponder this

God's master plan was that Abraham's descendants would be just like Abraham and make a big difference to a dark world, just as shining stars light up the night sky.

Do It Like This

As you know the human race kept messing up and making a disaster of the plan of the Master. So God decided to give them some practical guidelines on how they should live their lives. His instruction manual is called the Ten Commandments and in it God is saying, 'Listen folks, just do it like this.' In the next seven readings we will be unpacking God's ten golden rules and seeing how they could change the world.

22

Take this to heart

Read: Deuteronomy 6 verses 1–9

'Love the Lord your God with all your heart, with all your soul, and with all your strength. Never forget these commands that I am giving you today. Teach them to your children. Repeat them… when you are resting and when you are working.'

Deuteronomy 6:5–7

Before we plunge into the Ten Commandments we're going to look at the rule that sums all the others up. It's written in verse 5 and God wants us to take it to heart and never to forget it. He suggests writing it everywhere; on our wrists, on our forehead, our house and above all in our heart.

So start with the heart. Write it out here round the heart shape. Then write it on slips of paper and stick it on your notice board, your bedroom door, your watch and anywhere you will see it regularly. Think about it whenever you are in the bath, or waiting for the bus or doing the hoovering.

Ponder this

Ponder it now.

23

Worship me

Read: Deuteronomy 5 verses 1–11

The Lord said, 'I am the Lord your God, who rescued you from Egypt, where you were slaves. Worship no god but me.'

Deuteronomy 5:5–7

Everyone needs a reason to live and everyone, perhaps unconsciously, makes themselves a priority-list of things that they live for. Below on the right are some suggestions of the things that people live for. Try and put them in a top ten order of worthwhileness. Do add your own too.

Top ten in order	**Suggestions**
1	Being popular
2	Looking gorgeous
3	Having lots of money
4	Getting a good job
5	Doing your own thing
6	The opposite sex
7	Helping people
8	Having a family
9	Making a home
10	Other

Ponder this

From God's point of view the number one reason for our existence is that we be his friends; friends with the almighty, loving God of the universe. Even though the things on your list are mostly good in themselves, compared to living to be a friend of God they won't be as satisfying. That's why God spells out that we must put him first and worship him alone.

24

Holy-day

Read: Deuteronomy 5 verses 12–15

Observe the Sabbath and keep it holy, as I, the Lord your God have commanded you. You have six days in which to do your work, but the seventh day is a day of rest dedicated to me.

Deuteronomy 5:12–14

Jane and I were rather excited when we brought our first washing-machine a couple of years ago. We could now do our washing at home! The machine was well packaged when it arrived and came with all sorts of instruction manuals, explaining how to install and operate it. On this occasion I did read the instructions carefully before doing anything and it has worked fine ever since. But if I hadn't known to remove the polystyrene from the inside, or plumb in the 'dirty water out-flow pipe'—catastrophe!

God's guidelines for human life are just as practical. Take this one about having a day off each week. We all need a break every seven days, but more importantly it is vital that we have a special day when we can catch up with God after a busy week. So from now on why not decide to do all your weekend homework on Saturday and on Sunday take a ten-minute stroll, or sit down for a cup of tea and a chat with God. You'll find that you operate more smoothly after that!

Pray this

Why not talk to God about it now or write him an invitation for tea next Sunday?

25 ☐

What my m & d!?

Read: Deuteronomy 5 verse 16

'Respect your father and mother, as I, the Lord your God command you, so that all may go well with you and so that you may live a long time in the land that I am giving you.'

Deuteronomy 5:16

Hmmmmm! Look, we're all human, including your parents, and we all make mistakes. No, I'm not saying they made a mistake when they had you, but rather that nobody's perfect, so you need to make allowances for your mum and dad just as they probably make allowances for you. Anyway, respecting your father and mother, what does it mean? Tick your answers to the following questions.

- *Does it mean doing whatever they say even if it is 'unreasonable'?* Yes ☐ No ☐ Not sure ☐
- *Does it mean loving them?* Yes ☐ No ☐ Not sure ☐
- *Does it mean putting up with them?* Yes ☐ No ☐ Not sure ☐
- *Does it mean never saying what you think?* Yes ☐ No ☐ Not sure ☐
- *Does it mean taking a full page ad in the paper proclaiming how amazing your parents are?* Yes ☐ No ☐ Not sure ☐

Ponder this

If in doubt about what respecting YOUR parents in such-and-such a tricky situation means, try and imagine what Jesus would do at your age in your situation and you probably won't be far wrong.

P.S. I was not paid a huge sum of money by the 'Association of Parents of 11–14 Year Olds' to say all this.

And don't . . .

Read: Deuteronomy 5 verses 17–20

'Do not steal. Do not accuse anyone falsely.'

Deuteronomy 5:19–20

This all makes quite a lot of sense, doesn't it? No knotty problems to untangle here. Well, have you ever broken one of these two golden rules? Have you ever helped yourself to someone else's custard-flavour-extra-fizzy-sugar-bombs and then denied it saying, 'It weren't me, guv—it woz 'im'. Anyway, imagine that God has got your whole life on video (which I suppose he has in a funny kind of way). This one here contains the episode you were thinking of just now when you pinched something or blamed someone else. Label the video with a description of this incident (in code form if necessary).

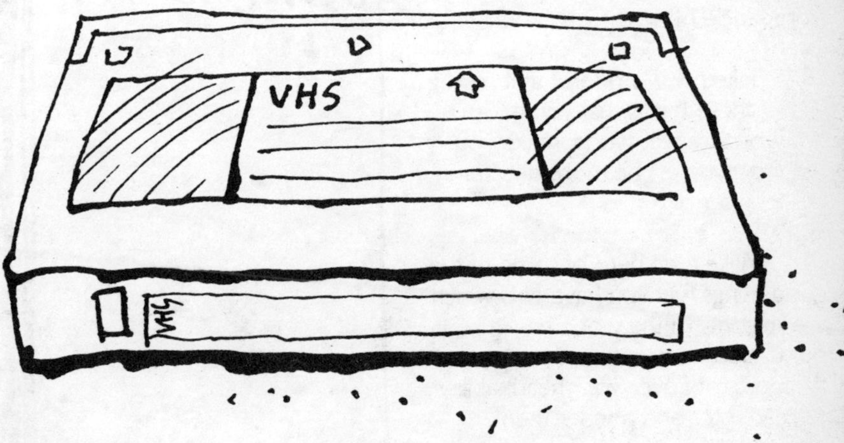

Ponder this

As you know, God saw it happen. So why not apologize to him and ask him to help you not to do it again? Once you've apologized he'll erase the incident once and for all. **Ponder this too:** *Is it appropriate to say sorry to the person you wronged? If it is, do it.*

27

Cooorrrwwh!

Read: Deuteronomy 5 verses 21–22

Do not desire another man's wife; do not desire his house, his land, his slaves, his cattle, his donkeys, or anything else that he owns.'

Deuteronomy 5:21

CD ROM, trendy parents, gorgeous hair, sense of humour, lovely body, super brain, happiness, latest outfits, just much nicer: they've got it and I want it. Do you know the feeling? It screws you up inside—wanting what you haven't got. Jealousy—it's like poison.

God doesn't recommend it. In fact it gets the big 'NO-NO'. But how do you stop yourself wanting what you haven't got? Well, here are some tips from Uncle Nick:

1 Take my word for it that having any of these things that you haven't got won't, repeat won't, make you the incy-winciest bit more happier in the long term.

2 Make a list here of some of the good things that you have got, which the majority of the world's population haven't, e.g. clean water to drink, roof over your head, ability to read, etc., and ponder them.

3 Remember that God really, really, really, really, really, really loves you just as you are. OK?

Pray this

Why not talk to God about this now?

If only . . .

Read: Deuteronomy 5 verse 1

'People of Israel, listen to all the laws that I am giving you today. Learn them and be sure that you obey them.'

Deuteronomy 5:1

If only everyone did listen to and obey God's very sensible guidelines then the world would be a very different place. Think of all the things that there would be no more of and add some of your own.

Pray this

Ask God to help you play your part in his plan by trying to follow his very sensible guidelines.

Out On Their Ear

I am very sorry to have to tell you that the descendants of Abraham didn't quite live up to God's expectations, despite the fact he had given them all those golden rules. By the year 597BC things had got rather desperate. The descendants of Abraham, living in Judah and Israel, had completely turned their backs on God. But they soon found out that you can't kick God in the teeth and get away with it. This week we shall find out how God dealt with them and managed to get at least some of them back on the straight and narrow.

Cause & effect

Read: 2 Kings 17 verses 7–12

The city of Samaria fell (to the Assyrian army) because the Israelites sinned against the Lord their God... They aroused the Lord's anger with all their wicked deeds and disobeyed the Lord's command not to worship idols.

2 Kings 17:7, 11–12

You can't kick God in the teeth and get away with it. You might well be able to kick a younger kid in the teeth and get away with it, or snub your family and get away with it, but you can't do it to God. The descendants of Abraham living in the city of Samaria found that out here. They ignored God's guidelines, did their own wicked thing and suffered the consequences in the form of the invading Assyrian army.

Every cause has its effect and every effect has its cause. If you insult your teacher you will get a detention; if you set fire to the carpet, the house will burn down. It's not the teacher's fault or the carpet's fault, it's your fault. Unfortunately the Israelites living in Samaria failed to realize that if they did evil then sooner or later they would reap the effects of their cause. It is not God's fault, it's just the way his universe works.

Pray this

Dear God please help me not to cause things that will affect others badly.

30

I did warn you

Read: 2 Kings 17 verses 13–18

The Lord had sent his messengers and prophets to warn Israel and Judah: 'Abandon your evil ways and obey my commands, which are contained in the Law I gave to your ancestors'... But they would not obey.

2 Kings 17:13–14

It is not as if God hadn't warned them. He sent them lots of messages through his prophets but the Israelites refused to listen to his advice.

Imagine that for some strange reason you suddenly had the urge to set off the school fire alarms. If you were lucky you just might get off with a caution—'Fire alarms are for emergencies and not for fun. Do you understand? Well, run along now and DON'T do it again.' The next time you couldn't resist that urge to smash the glass and hear the bell clattering away, you'd probably get a pretty stiff detention. If you did it a third time ('Oh, what a brilliant noise!') it's more than likely that you would have to take a 'compulsory break' from school. If you were stupid enough to take the hammer to the glass a fourth time you would be out on your ear for good.

It was like that with the Israelites. God warned them about their stupid and dangerous behaviour again and again and again. But they would not listen and in the end had to suffer the inevitable consequences of their disobedience, which was rather more than expulsion from school.

Ponder this

God is not to blame for the consequences of your actions.

Exiled

Read: 2 Chronicles 36 verses 11–21

The leaders of Judah, the priests, and the people followed the sinful example of the nations round them... So the Lord brought the king of Babylonia to attack them... He had no mercy on anyone... He burnt down the temple and the city... He took all the survivors to Babylonia.

2 Chronicles 36:14, 17, 19–20

The Israelites' next-door neighbours 'the Judahites' were also stupid enough to turn their backs on God and, as you might expect, suffered the inevitable consequences. King Nebuchadnezzar invaded, destroyed everything and took the survivors as slaves to Babylon.

As I have said many times already, everything that God does, he does because he loves us. 'But', I hear you think, 'what is loving about sending all your special people to be slaves to a foreign nation?' Well, God must have reckoned that he could still get the Judahites (or Jews as they were to be called) back on the straight and narrow and this was the way to do it. God's theory went like this: remove everything that they depend on (friends, home comforts, security, cultural trimmings) and they will realize that I'm all they've got left and I'm the only thing worth having. Well, it worked, surprise surprise, as we shall see tomorrow.

32

We're sorry

Read: Lamentations 3 verses 31–42

'Let us examine our ways and turn back to the Lord. Let us open our hearts to God in heaven and pray, "We have sinned and rebelled, and you, O Lord have not forgiven us."'

Lamentations 3:40–42

Today's reading is part of a poem written by one of the Jews in captivity in Babylon. God had finally got through to this person (huuurraaay!!). But, oh boy, did he have to use a sledgehammer to do it; prophets, the Babylonian army, and years in exile before they understood that he wasn't very happy with what they were up to.

Today God speaks to us in many different ways. He may give you good advice through your friends or family. He may speak to you in the words of the Bible or through your conscience (that little voice inside that makes you feel uneasy about something wrong that you are about to do). Draw an example of God speaking to someone through one of these four ways.

God speaks like this →

Pray this

Dear God, please help me to learn to hear what you want to say to me.

33

Hope

Read: Ezekiel 36 verses 22–32

'I will give you a new heart and a new mind. I will take away your stubborn heart of stone and give you an obedient heart. I will put my spirit in you and I will see to it that you follow my laws and keep all the commands I have given you.'

Ezekiel 36:26–27

Whist in exile in Babylon God had been working on the Jews (Judahites) through his prophet Ezekiel. God knew that they were seeing the light at last and so he promised them that he would wash them clean and help them to obey his laws! What a relief that must have been.

I find it pretty difficult to obey God's guidelines and do the things that he wants me to. OK, so I might not sacrifice my children to the sun, or worship horoscopes as the Judahites did, but being selfish, for example, comes pretty easily. The problem is my stubborn old heart which just doesn't have it in it to do what is right. God's promise of a new and obedient heart sounds almost too good to be true. But it is not, as we shall see later on.

For the moment devise a cinema advert for God's 'new hearts for old' promise.

Ponder this

Why not try to find out more about the product in your advert?

Dem bones

Read: Ezekiel 37 verses 1–14

God said to me, 'Mortal man, the people of Israel are like these bones. They say that they are dried up, without any hope... Tell them that... I will put my breath in them and bring them back to life, and let them live in their own land.'

Ezekiel 37:11–14

This is a groovy story illustrating what God was going to do for all his people living dried-up lives in Babylon. He was going to bring them to life!

Do you ever feel that something's wrong with your life? That it is not all that it could be? That it is a bit dry and dead? Well, God specialises in helping us to really live life to the full. Now grab your Bible, stand up and read the passage out loud with as much dramatic emphasis as you can possibly manage (without freaking out the neighbours).

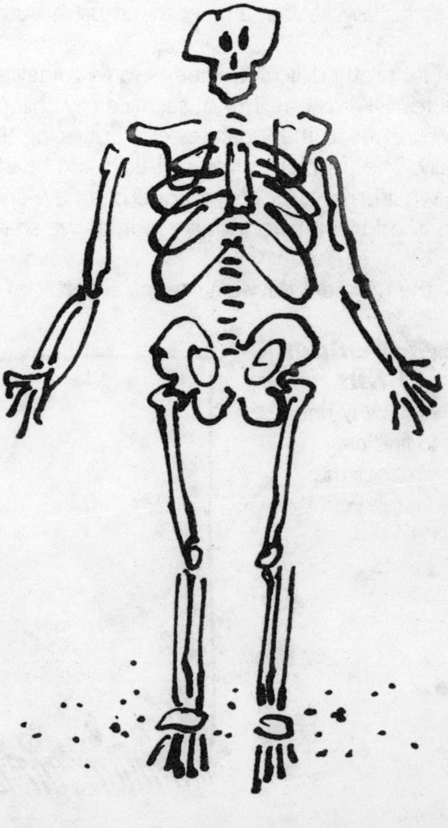

Ponder this

Sometimes the way in which we live our lives is like a dried-up skeleton compared to the full and exciting life that God wants us to have as his friends. Draw onto the skeleton some muscle, clothes and life and thank God that he wants to bring us to life in much the same way.

35

Happy ending

Read: 2 Chronicles 36 verses 22 & 23

In the first year that Cyrus of Persia was emperor (of Babylon) the Lord... prompted Cyrus to issue the following command... 'All of you who are God's people, go to Jerusalem, and may the Lord your God be with you.'

2 Chronicles 36:22–23

Seventy years after they were first captured and taken to Babylon God reckoned that the Jews had learnt their lesson and that they were ready to go home. So he got the new man in charge (good old Cyrus, emperor of the rapidly expanding Persian empire) to send them back to Jerusalem.

A happy ending! If it was a film you could imagine the final scene: the sun setting over a column of Judahites marching out across the desert. Stirring music fills the cinema as the credits move up the silver screen and the odd sniff is heard in the auditorium. If you were a film reviewer what would you say in your review about the plot of this film?

P.S. This is a true story and the events depicted took place between 597 and 538BC. Any resemblance between characters depicted and real people is entirely intended.

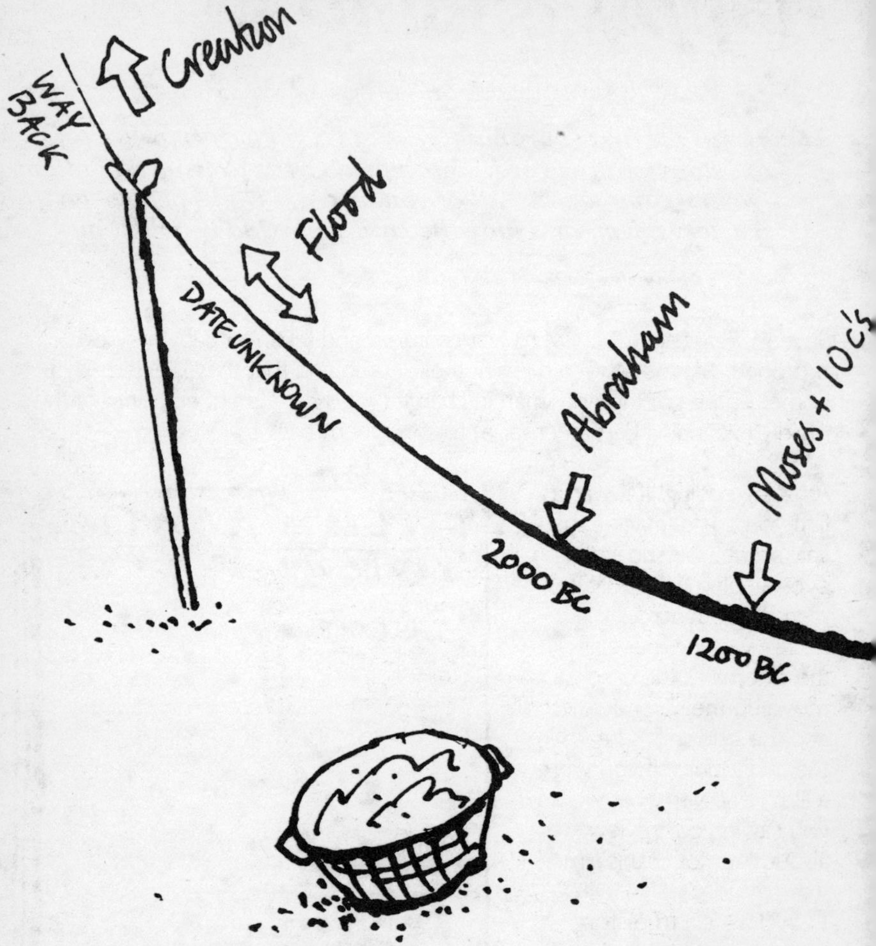
Creation
WAY BACK
Flood
DATE UNKNOWN
Abraham
2000 BC
Moses + 10c's
1200 BC

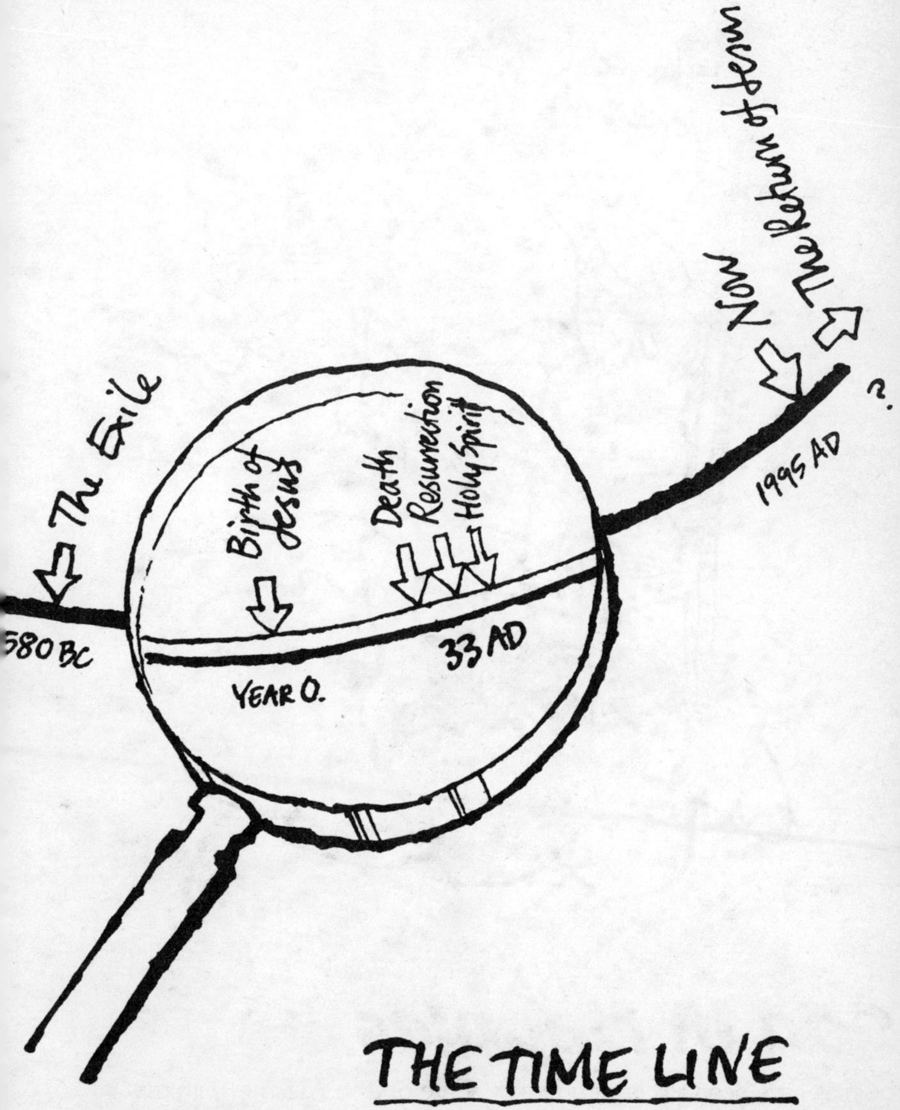

THE TIME LINE

P H A S E S I X

God In Nappies

You may have been a little surprised by some of God's dealings with us troublesome humans, but I guarantee you that the next phase of his master plan is the most astonishing yet. We've read his rules, heard his message, now prepare to meet the guy himself—in nappies.

The Master arrives

Read: Isaiah 9 verses 2, 6 & 7

The people who walked in darkness have seen a great light... A child is born to us! A son is given to us! And he will be our ruler. He will be called, 'Wonderful Counsellor', 'Mighty God', 'Eternal Father', 'Prince of Peace'.

Isaiah 9:2–6

God gave the guy who wrote these words a glimpse of the master stroke of his master plan eight centuries before the birth of Jesus. God was going to visit planet earth in human form, (... stunned silence). Can you imagine the excitement? God almighty coming to tea! No longer was he going to send messages through his prophets, no longer was he going to communicate from afar. He was going to arrive in person, tan tan tara!

Get your mind round that fact and write a newspaper headline announcing the imminent and greatest royal visit of history.

Ponder this

Even though the people of Israel had been expecting God's royal visit for 800 years most did not recognize him when he finally arrived.

Down to earth

Read: John 1 verse 14

The Word became a human being and, full of grace and truth, lived among us. We saw his glory, the glory which he received as the Father's only Son.

John 1:14

The first eighteen verses of John's gospel describe the theory of God's visit to planet earth, but you will probably need a little clue if you are to get it. Here's the clue and don't blink or you might miss it: the Word = Jesus. Read through the passage again changing 'the Word' to 'Jesus' and see what you get... God became a human being! Now there's a turn up for the books!

Try and completely fill up the human outline opposite with words that you feel describe God (e.g. loving, everlasting, mind-boggling, etc.)

Ponder this

When God became a human being in Jesus, his amazing 'God qualities' (see your list) became much more visible. Jesus is so perfectly the same as God in mind and behaviour that when we look at Jesus we see God. Mind-boggling!

I'll show you

Read: John 1 verse 18

No one has ever seen God. The only Son, who is the same as God and is at the Father's side, he has made him known.

John 1:18

Ever since the very first disaster that the Master had to face he has been working to get the human race back on the straight and narrow. You will remember how he washed out the evil in the human race and started again with Noah, and then again with Abraham. Despite giving clear guidelines on how to live, and teaching the people of Israel to love him during the exile in Babylon, human beings just couldn't live in the way that God wanted.

So God decided to come and show us how he wanted us to live. He became a human being and demonstrated what a real human life should be like. What a masterly plan! Now think about this:

- *How would you teach someone to draw a polar bear?*
- *How would you teach someone to use a computer?*

Well, if you were a good teacher you'd show them how; you would demonstrate. That's what God did when he became a man. He showed us how he wanted us to live.

Pray this

Why not thank God that he bothered to come and show us how to live?

Gob-smacked

Read: Luke 1 verses 26–38

The angel said to her, 'Don't be afraid, Mary; God has been gracious to you. You will become pregnant and give birth to a son, and you will name him Jesus. He will be great and will be called the Son of the Most High God.'

Luke 1:30–32

I expect Mary would have been gob- (or God-) smacked by this news. After all she was probably only fifteen or sixteen and had never had a boyfriend. She had been set up in this arranged marriage with this older man Joseph (nice bloke though I'm sure he was) and now she was pregnant and the father was God! In a way it would make quite a good plot for a comedy if it wasn't so serious...

Imagine yourself in Mary's shoes and scribble a letter to the problem page of her fav girl's magazine. Alternatively write a reply from the agony aunt to Mary's letter.

Ponder this

Once again God's doing things the hard way. Any idea why?

40

It's a boy!

Read: Luke 2 verses 1–20

An angel of the Lord appeared to the shepherds… They were terribly afraid, but the angel said to them, 'Don't be afraid! I am here with good news for you… This very day in David's town your Saviour was born—Christ the Lord!'

Luke 2:9–11

God certainly specializes in moving in mysterious ways. His only Son had just been born and he announced it first, not to the palace, but to a bunch of hairy shepherds. Often when people have a baby they send a card announcing the gory details to their friends. Imagine that you are God and fill in this card to tell the shepherds about the birth of your son. Add some suitable decorations too.

Ponder this

Why not send a card announcing the good news of God's arrival on planet earth to a friend? I suppose that's called a Christmas card, but who cares if it's June or September! The good news is for all year round.

Special baby

Read: Luke 2 verses 22–38

Simeon took the child in his arms and gave thanks to God: 'Now. Lord, you have kept your promise... With my own eyes I have seen your salvation.'

Luke 2:28–30

Nine months previously the angel had given Mary the first information about her rather special baby (day 39). Today she gets quite a bit more coded info from this guy Simeon. Jot down some of the things that the angel, shepherds and Simeon have told her about her baby.

Now do a bit of detective work and try and sum up in less than fifteen words what Mary knew about her child.

....

....

Growing up

Read: Luke 2 verses 39& 40

The child grew and became strong; he was full of wisdom, and God's blessings were upon him.

Luke 2:40

I find the thought of God almighty being a human being quite astonishing, particularly when I think of God in nappies, or God being breast-fed or eating chips. (Okay, so maybe he didn't eat chips, but you know what I mean.) Jesus' childhood would have been pretty similar to the experience of the majority of children round the world.

Ponder this

Think about your average day from when you get up to when you go to bed and jot down some of the things that you have to do. Then write the words 'Jesus did this too' opposite each thing you think he would have done.

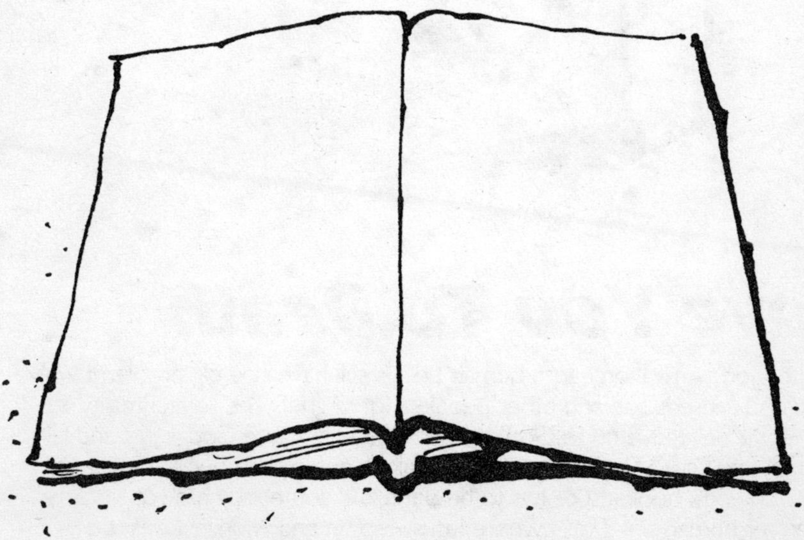

Love You To Death

Despite God's arrival on earth, human beings still have one big problem: we've sinned and caused God and other people a lot of grief. The painful reality is that we will never live up to God's standards and because God is just and fair he simply can't say, 'There, there, never mind!' and sweep our sin under the carpet. In God's book justice has to be done and somebody has got to carry the can for human sin. That's where Jesus steps in and willingly takes the blame. His death is the ultimate sacrifice and the ultimate solution to our problems. Prepare to find out how and why.

43

Revealed

Read: Romans 3 verses 21–26

Now God's way of putting people right with himself has been revealed... God puts people right through their faith in Jesus Christ.

Romans 3:21–22

Yesterday I was reading a Greenpeace campaign report. They had just revealed, in their typically spectacular way, a new supermarket freezer that doesn't use chemicals that destroy the ozone layer or cause global warming: an exciting solution to some of our environmental problems.

Two thousand years ago God revealed his solution to the massive problem of human sin and guilt—nothing other than Jesus Christ.

Design an advertising catch-phrase or slogan for God's ultimate solution to our personal problems.

In case you were wondering

We will be thinking about why and how Jesus is the solution over the next few days so don't worry if it doesn't make sense yet.

Sin to death

Read: Romans 6 verse 23

Sin pays its wage—death; but God's free gift is eternal life in union with Christ Jesus our Lord.

Romans 6:23

One of the basic laws of God's universe is that rejecting God (otherwise known as 'sin') leads to the death of our relationship with him. It's pretty obvious really. Think of it like this: if you continually hurt or never bothered to visit or talk to one of your friends or relatives then your relationship would die. It is like that with us and God except that every single person has turned their back on God and hurt him badly. The relationship with God is dead…

BUT

God's free gift to each person who wants it, is eternal and wonderful life with him through Jesus. We don't deserve it but the plan of the Master is for us to have it. Good news or what?!

Ponder this

Do you want God's free gift?

Yes ☐ No ☐ Not sure ☐

Why not talk to him about it?

Love you to death

Read: Romans 5 verses 6–11

God has shown us how much he loves us—it was while we were still sinners that Christ died for us! By his blood we are now put right with God.

Romans 5:8–9

Rescue me

Read: John 10 verses 7–18

Jesus said, 'I am the good shepherd who is willing to die for the sheep.'

John 10:11

A couple of years ago Jane and I walked from Glasgow to Fort William along the West Highland Way. At one of the farm houses where we stayed we were told about a shepherd who had drowned that winter in the swollen river that ran down the valley. One of his sheep had fallen in and the shepherd died saving it.

Imagine that you're a sheep. How would knowing that you had a top quality shepherd to look after you make you feel? Fill in the bubble with your thoughts.

Ponder this

You and I are like sheep and Jesus is our shepherd. He cares about us so much that he was prepared to give up his life in order to make sure that we are safe. How does this make you feel? Why not talk to him about it?

‘Crucify him!’

Read: John 18 verse 38—John 19 verse 16

Pilate said to the people, ‘Here is your king!’ They shouted back, ‘Kill him! Kill him! Crucify him!’

John 19:14–15

Hearing about miscarriages of justice on the news makes me really angry. When I read about the trial of Jesus I feel a strange mixture of emotions. On the one hand I get really angry at the horrific injustice of what is happening to Jesus. On the other I am aware that Jesus has made a choice to go through with it all because of me; to take the punishment that I deserve for neglecting God. It is a case of God, once again, working out his perfect master plan despite human disasters.

Think through the events of this passage from some of the following people's points of view and write a quote that sums up their feelings.

“ .... ”

Pilate

“ .... ”

Crowds

“ .... ”

Soldiers

“ .... ”

Chief Priests

“ .... ”

Jesus

“ .... ”

You

Murdered

Read: John 19 verses 16–37

Jesus knew that by now everything had been completed... he bowed his head and died.

John 19:28, 30

Over the last few days we have been thinking about why Jesus died and what his death achieved. Today we're looking at the raw facts of the crucifixion. When I read about Jesus' death I sometimes take it for granted because it's so familiar. At other times I'm shocked by the horror of it all.

When I see photographs of the dead bodies of the murdered victims of the war in Bosnia or Rwanda they bring home to me the reality of what happened to Jesus. The crucifixion isn't a fairy story, or a nice idea for a bit of jewellery, but a bloody and violent murder. It was a horrific event that God turned round and made into the means of our being put right with him.

Ponder this

Here is a drawing of the crucifixion. Where do you stand in relation to Jesus? Are you throwing dice with the soldiers, kneeling at his feet, looking on from a distance or completely off the page? Draw yourself in and talk to him about it.

Tons of love

Read: John 3 verse 16

God loved the world so much that he gave his only Son, so that everyone who believes in him may not die but have eternal life.

John 3:16

Well, this verse sums up God's rescue plan for the human race beautifully. It tells us what God did, why he did it, what we have to do and what happens when we do it. Neat, eh?! Seriously though, if you take the message of this verse on board you will have understood the main plan of the Master in the face of disaster. Fill in the luggage and then take it on board your life.

Pray this

Thank God for his never ending and very practical love for you.

P H A S E   E I G H T

Death Defeated

It has probably occurred to you that the master stroke of God's master plan was perhaps a little odd. After all, it did involve getting himself killed! 'Great!' I hear you think. 'Where does that leave us?' Well, he didn't stay dead for long—about a day and a half to be precise. The resurrection of Jesus is God's way of showing that he gave Jesus the thumbs up for his part in his master plan. Jesus' death in our place has been approved as God's official means of salvation for human beings.

50

Gone

Read: John 20 verses 1–10

Then Peter and the other disciple went to the tomb… He saw the linen wrappings lying there and the cloth which had been round Jesus' head.

John 20:3, 6–7

Two days after the crucifixion Jesus' body had gone. There was no doubt about it—Jesus' body was not in the tomb. So where on earth was it? Or was it not on earth at all? Perhaps it had gone 'out of this world'! Well, over the centuries people have suggested various possible explanations. Here are some of them:

1. **The disciples went to the wrong tomb**—nice try, but would you forget where your best friend was buried?—probably not!

2. **The disciples stole the body and then pretended Jesus was alive**—*the thing is they just weren't that cool. They were a bunch of nervous wrecks after the crucifixion.*

3. **The Jews stole the body**—*well, if they had they would have produced it in a flash in order to disprove the disciples' claim that Jesus was alive.*

4. **Jesus didn't actually die on the cross. He just passed out and came round in the tomb** —*dream on! I mean have you ever seen a crucifixion? And, by the way, he was lying in a cold tomb not in an intensive care bed.*

Well, at this point in the story all they knew was that Jesus' body was not in the tomb. You will have to wait till tomorrow to find out what happened next.

It's me!

Read: John 20 verses 11–18

Mary turned round and saw Jesus standing there.

John 20:14

There is a brilliant moment in Nick Park's Oscar-winning animated film *The Wrong Trousers* when Wallace suddenly recognizes that the armed robber 'chicken' who has taken him prisoner is in fact the penguin who has been renting a room in his house. Wallace can't believe whom he's just recognized.

When Mary recognizes that the man she is talking to is her beloved master she is completely overwhelmed. Try and imagine some of the thoughts that would have raced through her mind in that wonderful moment. Jot them in the flash below.

Ponder this

Jesus chose to make his first resurrection appearance to little ol' Mary Magdalene who most important people wouldn't have passed the time of day with. What matters to Jesus is not how important we are, but how much we love him.

Right lads

Read: John 20 verses 19–23

It was late that Sunday evening, and the disciples were gathered together behind locked doors... Then Jesus came and stood among them... The disciples were filled with joy at seeing the Lord.

John 20:19–20

One thing is sure—the disciples weren't expecting the events described here to happen. They knew that Jesus' body had gone and Mary had told them that she had seen him alive, but they didn't really understand what was going on. They were very frightened that they'd be next on the Jewish authorities' hit list. Then Jesus broke into their fear-filled get-together.

Plot a graph of the disciples' changing heart-rate over the verses of this passage. (Your heart-rate goes up when you are very stressed, frightened, excited or exercising and down when you are very relaxed, asleep or dead.)

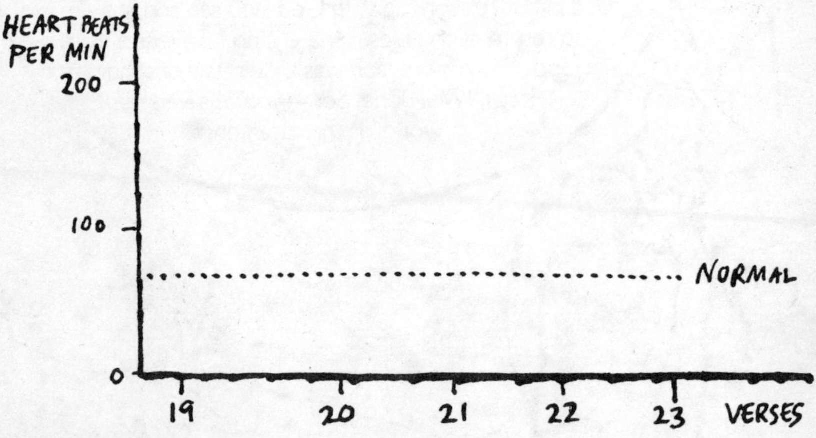

Ponder this

Ponder the joy that the disciples must have felt when they saw Jesus alive again. It must have been the best Easter present that God could possibly have given them.

Put right

Read: Romans 4 verse 25

Because of our sins Jesus was handed over to die, and he was raised to life in order to put us right with God.

Romans 4:25

Ponder this

No resurrection—no hope—no forgiveness—no Christianity.

54 ☐

Believe it

Read: John 20 verses 24–29

Jesus said to Thomas, 'Do you believe because you see me? How happy are those who believe without seeing me!'

John 20:29

The death and resurrection of Jesus are the crunch events in God's master plan for the human race. Only through the death and resurrection of Jesus can the disaster we have made of our relationship with God be put right. However, we have to play our part in the plan of the Master. The death and resurrection of Jesus will only put you right with God if you accept it for yourself. That's what Thomas discovered here.

How do you feel about God's master plan for putting right your relationship with him?

COMPLETELY CONVINCED ☐ *It's brilliant, it's worked for me and I love him loads.*

WORKING OK ☐ *I know it's true and I've accepted it for myself but sometimes I do have my doubts.*

YES PLEASE ☐ *It kind of makes sense now and I want my friendship with God to be put right today.*

NOT SURE REALLY ☐ *Well, it sounds interesting but I don't feel ready yet. Give me a bit more time.*

GIVE ME A BREAK ☐ *Look, it's fine for you, but it doesn't make any sense to me.*

Pray this

Whichever box you have ticked why not talk to God about how you feel and what you should do next.

55

Life plan

Read: John 20 verses 30–31

These [accounts] have been written in order that you may believe that Jesus is the Messiah, the Son of God, and that through your faith in him you may have life.

John 20:31

Dear Reader

This seemed as good a moment as any to write you a letter. I've found thinking about the plan of the Master in the face of disaster fascinating and have been very struck by the way in which God does everything because of his enormous love for us. This verse sums it up nicely. God wants us to have '*Life*' and believing in Jesus gives us '*Life*'—with a capital '*L*' in italics!

God's master plan for you and me is for us to be really alive—living life to the full. Since I asked Jesus to become involved in my day-to-day living back in 1981 my life has really taken off. I don't mean that I have become an international celebrity, but rather that I know that God loves me and I now have a very good reason to be alive. That makes a massive difference.

Accepting the death and resurrection of Jesus for yourself really does bring new Life. Do try it!

P.S. *Perhaps you could talk to a Christian friend or youth group leader about this.*

Nick

Dead—not for long

Read: Acts 2 verses 22–24

'In accordance with his own plan God had already decided that Jesus would be handed over to you; and you killed him... But God raised Jesus from death, setting him free from its power, because it was impossible that death should hold him prisoner.'

Acts 2:23–24

On the blackboard below make a list of things that are totally impossible. For example: a cat giving birth to puppies, or a mushroom turning into a Rolls Royce.

Ponder this

Just as the things on your list are completely impossible it was impossible for Jesus, the Son of God, to stay dead.

Fired Up

Forty days after Jesus' resurrection he returned to heaven to be with God. But before he went he promised his followers that he would send his Holy Spirit to be with each one of them as their helper.

Now, as far as God is concerned the problem with the human race is that they just can't seem to do what's right. Or put it this way: doing the wrong thing comes more easily than doing the right. It is not that we don't know the difference between right and wrong, it's just that we've got a natural flair for the wrong. What we need is a change of heart and a change of heart is what God has made possible by sending his Holy Spirit to help us live for him. His 'new heart' treatment makes all the difference.

The promised gift

Read: Acts 1 verses 1–5

For 40 days after his death Jesus appeared to his disciples many times... He gave them this order... 'Wait for the gift I told you about, the gift my Father promised... in a few days you will be baptised with the Holy Spirit.'

Acts 1:3–5

The prospect of being given a present can be very exciting, particularly so when you have an idea that the present is something you really want. For Christmas last year a friend gave me a map of the part of the Lake District where Jane and I were going on holiday. I was really excited about getting the map because it held the promise of the holiday to come. We could look at it and plan all the walks we were going to do. How do you feel when you are lying awake on Christmas Eve? Jot your thoughts round the picture.

After his resurrection Jesus told his disciples that God was going to send them an extraordinary present; a gift that would totally transform their lives. They would be filled with God's Holy Spirit. I'm not sure that they understood what Jesus was talking about, but if they knew what we know about the Holy Spirit today, they wouldn't have been able to sleep, think straight or do anything else because of the excitement.

Ponder this

Sometimes things we look forward to can turn out to be a disappointment, but the gift of the Holy Spirit will never disappoint us because he is part of the Master's plan for our lives and the Master knows best.

58

Gift day

Read: Acts 2 verses 1–12

When the day of Pentecost came, all the believers were gathered together in one place… They were all filled with the Holy Spirit and began to talk in other languages, as the Spirit enabled them to speak.

Acts 2:1, 4

All the disciples were together when the moment came for God to hand over his gift. Oh boy, did they know something special had happened! They found that they could speak with people in languages they had never heard before. (I wonder if this is not another classic case of God doing things the hard way?) Anyway, let's deal with another question and answer before we go any further.

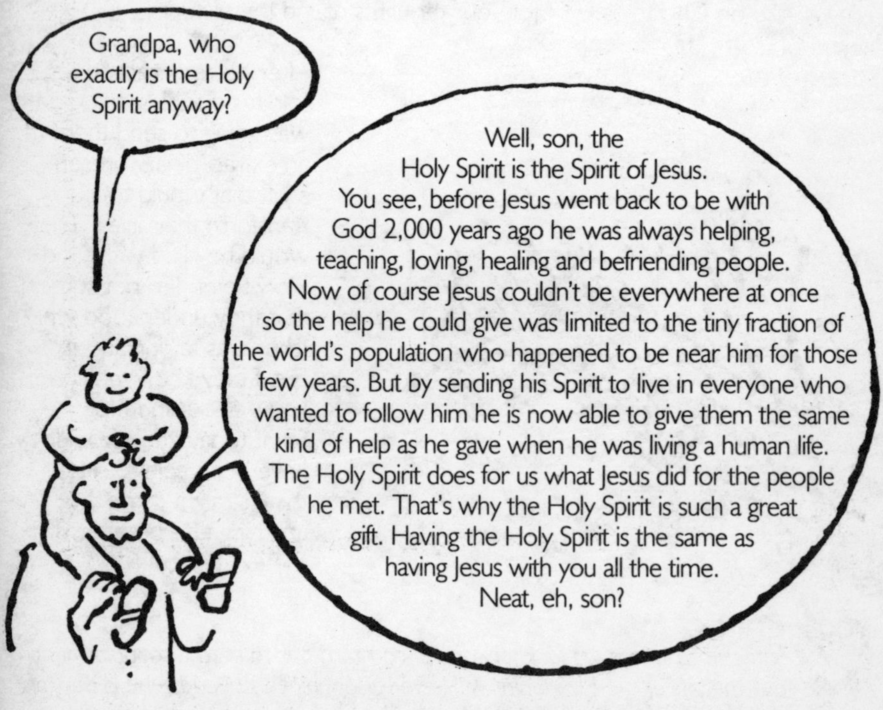

Open to all

Read: Acts 2 verses 14–21

Peter began to speak to the crowd... 'This is what the prophet Joel spoke about: 'This is what I will do in the last days, God says: "I will pour out my Spirit on everyone."''

Acts 2:14–17

The special offer of God's gift, the Holy Spirit, is for absolutely everyone: young, old, tall, short, and all the in-betweens. The only requirement is that you have to want him to be part of your life. (Obviously he won't force his way in if you really and definitely don't want anything to do with God!)

Fill out this ad with the details that you know about God's special offer of the Holy Spirit.

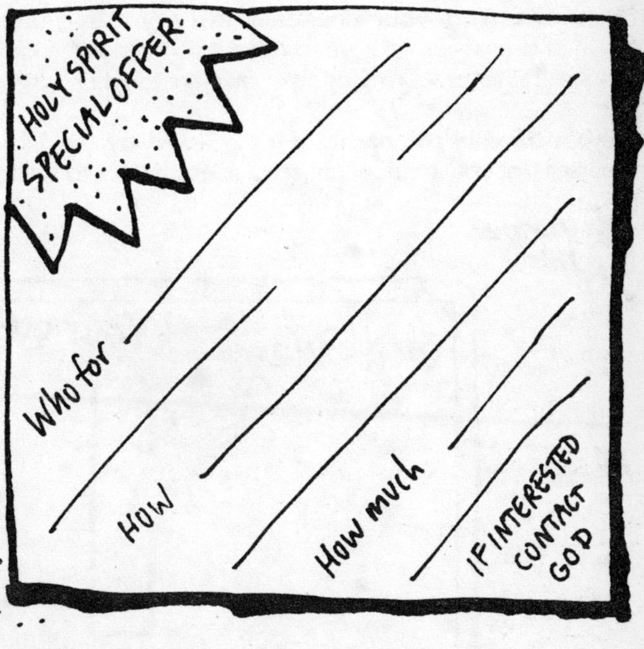

Ponder this

Do you want to accept God's special offer and have the Spirit of Jesus come and live in you and give you the help that Jesus gave his friends 2,000 years ago? Why not talk to him about how you feel?

Instructions please

Read: Acts 2 verses 36–42

Peter said to the crowd, 'Each one of you must turn away from your sins and be baptised in the name of Jesus Christ, so that your sins will be forgiven; and you will receive God's gift, the Holy Spirit.'

Acts 2:38

In this passage Peter explains how to switch from following your own life plan to God's master plan. There are two simple steps to take and they lead to the gift of eternal life (with the Holy Spirit thrown in free).

1. Turn away from your sins—well, that is obvious enough. But it is not a question of cleaning up your life to make it good enough for God, for that is impossible, rather of telling God that you want to go his way.

2. Be baptized in the name of Jesus—well, this is a public way of saying for yourself that you are now on Jesus' side and want to live for him.

Ponder this

On the road sign jot down a few of the attractions of 'Your way' and 'God's way' and weigh them up for yourself.

What a change . . .

Read: Acts 2 verses 43–47

Many miracles and wonders were being done through the apostles, and everyone was filled with awe. All the believers continued together in close fellowship and shared their belongings with one another.

Acts 2:43–44

The disciples, who only a few weeks before were nervous wrecks, were now out and about performing miracles right, left and centre. Everyone who joined them became like one big family. 'Hmmmm,' thought the crack reporter from the *Jerusalem Times*, 'something fishy is going on here.' Well, it is called the Holy Spirit at work, making people like Jesus.

Now, when the Holy Spirit gets to work in your life, you will change too. Don't worry if your experience is not as dramatic as that of those first Christians—you will still be changing.

Think of one area of your life that the Holy Spirit might want to change so that you are more like Jesus. Write it here.

....

....

Pray this

Why not ask the Holy Spirit to help you become more like Jesus in that area of your life? He'll be delighted to help because that's his job.

Playing their part

Read: Acts 4 verses 23–31

When they finished praying, the place where they were meeting was shaken. They were all filled with the Holy Spirit and began to proclaim God's message with boldness.

Acts 4:31

Prepare to be mind-boggled. A more astonishing fact than this you may never hear… *(fanfare)*… Did you know… *(sharp intake of breath)*… that God *(gasp)* wants to use **you** to carry out his master plan for the human race? *(thud)* Now wake up, because he does, and that fact is in itself part of his master plan.

God has decided to use little old us (puny as we may feel) to change this world for the better. That is what these first Christians were doing here. They were talking to God about what he wanted them to do and asking him to give them the strength to do it. And with the help of the Holy Spirit they did it.

Pray this

Get yourself comfy, close your eyes and ask God what part he wants you to play in his master plan today. Then sit quietly and see what comes into your mind. You might think of someone at school who is very unhappy—perhaps you could speak to them. Maybe it will be a question of apologizing to someone you have hurt. Whatever it is ask the Holy Spirit to help you do it.

63

New hearts for old

Read: Ezekiel 36 verses 26 & 27

The Lord said, 'I will give you a new heart and a new mind. I will take away your stubborn heart of stone and give you an obedient heart. I will put my spirit in you and I will see to it that you follow my laws.'

Ezekiel 36:26–27

Throughout the history of the world the main disaster God has had to deal with is the tendency of the human heart to disobey him. Now cast your mind back to day 33 when we saw how God promised the Jews living in exile in Babylon that one day he would replace their stubborn hearts with obedient ones. Well, that is the job of the Holy Spirit and he is now busy softening our stubborn hearts, turning them into obedient ones. Thank God.

Next to each of the stony hearts below list one of the ways in which you are hard-hearted towards God or other people (e.g. selfish, uncaring, proud).

Pray this

Choose one of the hard hearts and ask the Holy Spirit to slowly and surely soften it, reshape it, warm it up and turn it into a pumping, caring, obedient, loving and generous heart.

PHASE TEN

Finishing The Job

Jesus, the Son of God, arrived on planet earth in human form for the first time 2,000 years ago. The Bible tells us that at some point in the future he will come back in style to end the world as we know it, finish off evil and bring all God's friends to be with him in paradise. This is a very important part of the Christian faith because it is the final masterly stroke of God's master plan for the human race. The New Testament alone mentions the return of Jesus more than 250 times. Over the next week we will be exploring some of the things that it tells us about what will happen when Jesus comes back and how we can help God clinch his master plan for the human race.

I'll be back

Read: Matthew 24 verses 29–31

Jesus said, 'Then the sign of the Son of Man will appear in the sky; and all the peoples of the earth will weep as they see the Son of Man coming on the clouds of heaven with power and great glory.'

Matthew 24:30

The first thing to say about the return of Jesus is that it will be very dramatic. There will be sensational cosmic phenomena in the sky and every person who is alive will see Jesus—it'll be the end of the world as we know it.

When I think about the state of the world—all the hatred, injustice, wars and poverty, not to mention all the nuclear weapons knocking about the planet—I have a horrible sense of looming disaster. But that is NOT God's way of thinking about the events of human history. God is not going to let the human race wipe itself out in an unfortunate nuclear catastrophe—***he*** is going to end it at the correct moment in his master plan. I find this very reassuring and I need to remind myself of it often!

Ponder this

The return of Jesus to sort out the world once and for all is something to look forward to! You may not be convinced of that yet, but hopefully by the end of the week you will be. Jot down your feelings about the return of Jesus and the end of the world here.

....

....

....

The E.T.A.

Read: Matthew 24 verses 36–41

Jesus said, 'No one knows, however, when that day and hour will come—neither the angels in heaven nor the Son; the Father alone knows.'

Matthew 24:36

Jesus' answer to the question 'When's your ETA (expected time of arrival)?' was NOK (no one knows). No one knows when he will be coming back to end the world. So there is not much we can do about it. Or is there?

This reminds me of a story about a man who went to a Jewish Rabbi and asked when he should repent and turn to God. The Rabbi replied that he should do it on the very last day of his life; then he could enjoy doing his own thing every day of his life and still be right with God when he died. 'But, Rabbi,' the man asked, 'how do I know which is my last day?' The Rabbi replied, 'If you don't know when you are going to die then you'd better turn to God right now.'

As you don't know when Jesus is going to come back, or when you are going to die, or which will be first, any wise old sage with half a brain in his head would give you this advice, 'Get straight with God now.'

Ponder this

Is there anything you need to talk over with God now? Why not sit down, make a list and then have a word with him about it?

66

On your toes

Read: Matthew 25 verses 14–30

Jesus said, 'At that time the Kingdom of heaven will be like this. Once there was a man who was about to go on a journey; he called his servants and put them in charge of his property… After a long time the master of those servants came back and settled accounts with them.'

Matthew 25:14, 19

If you knew that Jesus was going to return to end history as we know it at precisely 9.04 a.m. tomorrow morning, what difference would it make to what you did today? Jot your thoughts down here.

Ponder this

Since we don't know when Jesus will return, he advises us to be always ready. Today's passage explains how we can do just that. In Jesus' story the master gives his servants gifts to manage. Two of them try hard to make the most of their gifts and the master is pleased with them when he returns. The third servant can't be bothered and ends up in deep water. The point Jesus is making is that being ready for his return is simply a question of doing our best for him now. How can you do your best for Jesus today? Fill in the date in the calendar, jot down your thoughts and talk to God about them.

The J day

Read: Acts 17 verses 30–31

Paul said, 'God has overlooked the times when people did not know him, but now he commands all of them everywhere to turn away from their evil ways. For he has fixed a day in which he will judge the whole world with justice.'

Acts 17:30–31

When was the last time you were treated unfairly? Maybe you were blamed for something that you hadn't done or someone was horrible to you for no good reason. Write it here. How did it make you feel?

....

When unfair things happen to people I care about I get really angry. However, my feelings are nothing compared to the pain and hurt of the millions of people round the world who suffer much more serious injustice: torture, famine, poverty, cruelty. God feels that pain infinitely more than we ever can and one day he is going to bring justice to the world. The people who have caused others to suffer will be dealt with and all wrongs will be put right once and for all. WOW!—that is a day to look forward to!

Ponder this

God wants to use you to help bring justice to his world. This is not so that you pass the Big Judgement Day Test (Jesus has passed it for us already, thank God—see day 45) but in order to make life better for others and please God. Doing what God wants us to now is how we help him clinch his master plan once and for all. Look back to day 62. What did you think God wanted you to do? Did you do it and what happened? Why not talk to him about it and ask him what he wants you to do now?

Devil destroyed

Read: Revelation 20 verse 10

Then the Devil, who deceived them, was thrown into the lake of fire and sulphur.

Revelation 20:10

I haven't really mentioned the devil up to now, but he has played a pretty big part in causing disasters for the Master to deal with. In fact, right from Day One the devil has been waging war against God and his master plan. It is also pretty obvious, looking at all the hate and evil in the world, that he has been rather successful in his battle. But when Jesus comes back he will destroy the devil once and for all. Now, there is something to look forward to!

In the box below make a list of some of the bad and evil things that happen in the world.

Pray this

When Jesus comes back all these things that you have written will be destroyed and will never happen again. As a symbol of this tear the bottom half of this page out of the book, shred it and throw it away. As you do so thank Jesus that one day he is going to deal finally with evil.

69

Wooowee!

Read: Revelation 21 verses 1–7

'Now God's home is with human beings! He will live with them, and they shall be his people… He will wipe away all tears from their eyes. There will be no more death, no more grief or crying or pain. The old things have disappeared.'

Revelation 21:3–4

The plan of the Master has at last come full circle. Originally God intended every human being to be his friend, but as you know we all went a bit off the rails. But when Jesus comes again everyone who has been put right with God through the death of Jesus will be with him in paradise. Wooowee!

I long for that day because my struggle to do the right thing will be over and so will all the things that spoil life. We will be changed to be like Jesus and be the kind of people that God originally intended. Woooweee again! No more death, tears, pain, sin... What a prospect!

C.S. Lewis in the last couple of paragraphs of his last Narnia book gives us a glimpse of how exciting heaven will be. Here it is for you to read. The children have just arrived in Narnia for the last time after having been killed in a railway accident.

> Aslan turned to them and said: 'You do not yet look so happy as I mean you to be.'
>
> Lucy said, 'We're so afraid of being sent away, Aslan. And you have sent us back into our own world so often.'
>
> 'No fear of that,' said Aslan. 'Have you not guessed?'
>
> Their hearts leaped and a wild hope rose within them.
>
> 'There was a real railway accident,' said Aslan softly. 'Your father and mother and all of you are—as you used to call it in the Shadowlands—dead. The term is over: the holidays have begun. The dream is ended: this is the morning.'
>
> And as he spoke He no longer looked to them like a lion; but the things that began to happen after that were so great and beautiful that I cannot write them. And for us this is the end of all the stories, and we can most truly say that they lived happily ever after. But for them it was only the beginning of the real story. All their life in this world and all their adventures in Narnia had only been the cover and the title page: now at last they were beginning Chapter One of the Great Story which no one on earth has read: which goes on for ever: in which every chapter is better than the one before.

C.S. Lewis, *The Last Battle*, published by HarperCollins © 1956

Ponder this

Read the Bible passage again remembering that our life on this earth is only the cover and the title page of the 'real story' that begins when we join God in heaven. There every chapter is better than the one before.

With God

Read: Revelation 22 verses 1–5

The throne of God... will be in the city, and his servants will worship him. They will see his face.

Revelation 22:3–4

Do you ever imagine your absolute hero coming to stay with you? Or better still going to stay with them? Ryan Giggs, Keanu Reeves, Picasso—imagine it! What would you do together? Stay up chatting all night, kick a ball about for a bit, go to the club for a drink or paint a picture? Actually, it would probably get a bit difficult after a while. But never mind, nice thought.

Ponder this

Now try and imagine seeing God face to face and living in his house! Pheweee! Now, that would be something. The difference would be that this guy, as well as being the mind-blowingly amazing King of the universe, actually really loves you and is thrilled to have you around.

Why not write to him and explain how you feel about the prospect of living with him in paradise for ever?

Now look back to day 64 and see if your feelings about the end of the world have changed at all.

Dear God
About paradise...

A last letter

Dear Reader

Well done! You have finished your epic journey through the plan of the Master in the face of disaster—quite an achievement. To help you see what you have learnt here are some final questions for you to ponder.

1. What have you discovered about God in the last ten weeks?

....

....

2. What have you learnt about your self? ....

....

3. What difference will all this make to your life?...............

....

....

Pray this

Why don't you spend some time talking to God about what you have discovered and the effect that he wants it to have on you?

Nick

What next?

If you have enjoyed these
'Lightning Bolts' daily readings
why not get yourself another set?

Other Lightning Bolts Titles

Struck by Jesus

Struck by Jesus is your chance to read through Mark's Gospel in seventy days and discover what it was that made Jesus so different.

Getting to Grips with God

Getting to Grips with God will help you grapple with the ten crunch questions about the Christian faith, from 'Does God exist?' through to 'Why should I be a Christian and what would it involve anyway?'

Struck by Jesus is available now,
and *Getting to Grips with God* is
published in the spring of 1996.

Both titles are available from your local Christian bookshop
or, in case of difficulty, direct from BRF,
Peter's Way, Sandy Lane West, Oxford OX4 5HG.
Telephone BRF (01865) 748227 to confirm prices.
BRF is a Registered Charity.